For my special little people Ethan and Elena Croucher
who gave me all sorts of wonderful tips
during the painting of this story

Text and illustrations copyright © Christina Balit 2021
First published in Great Britain and in the USA in 2021 by
Otter-Barry Books, Little Orchard, Burley Gate, Herefordshire, HR1 3QS
www.otterbarrybooks.com

ISBN 978-1-91307-472-2

Illustrated with watercolours
Set in Gotham Book

Printed in China
9 8 7 6 5 4 3 2 1

THE
CORINTHIAN GIRL

Champion Athlete of Ancient Olympia

Christina Balit

Otter-Barry BOOKS

THERE WAS ONCE A GIRL who was given no name. She lived long ago in Athens, the greatest and most important city in the world. Gods lived on the mountaintops, nymphs protected the trees and the Goddess Athena guarded over all. But a girl who had no name was of no importance and even the Gods didn't notice her.

Everyone called her 'The Corinthian girl' because Corinth was where she came from. She was strong but very quiet. She was tall but very shy. She lived in the kitchen of a large brick house under the shadow of the Acropolis. She cleaned the house and washed its walls. She scrubbed its floors and swept its tiles.

She barely spoke because she was not allowed to. She was a slave and a slave had no need for words. But the Corinthian girl had not been born a slave....

Ten days after her birth, her father did what all fathers must do. He walked to the steps of the Temple with his baby in his arms to take part in a special ceremony, to choose whether or not he would give her a name and the right to be a citizen of the city.

All fathers had to make this choice and it wasn't easy. If he decided that his family was already too large, he could give his child away forever. This child was a girl. A girl was expensive. A girl would need a dowry one day and he couldn't afford that.

So the father turned from the Temple and walked to the marketplace instead.

He pushed through quarrelling tradesmen and customers bartering in the busy stalls. He found an empty stone bench beside an old carthorse and dancing clowns trying to earn a living. There he placed his baby girl for all to see, hoping that someone might have need of her and take her away. A childless couple perhaps? A merchant in need of a young slave to sew and pick vegetables?

He tied a small copper Doric coin round her neck to show that she was from a strong and worthy family. At worst, someone would throw her to the bottom of a disused well for the Gods to deal with. Her death would not be his responsibility.

Everyone had the right to dispose of an unneeded child. And a girl was the most unneeded of them all.

Wrapped tightly in her swaddling rags, the baby cried and cried.

Nobody likes a crying infant and most of the passing tradesmen ignored her and walked past. Eventually she became quiet and still. A dog walked by and sniffed her in case she promised to be a tasty snack. An old fisherman picked her up to feel her weight and study her tiny face for any imperfections.

Eventually an elderly slave from Athens poked the baby with his stick and she gurgled. This made him smile, so he checked her hands and feet in case she was missing any fingers or toes. Happy that she seemed to be healthy, he gathered her into his basket and carried her home to his Master's house in far-off Athens.

The child wouldn't be of much use to him now, but in a few years he could easily put her to work.

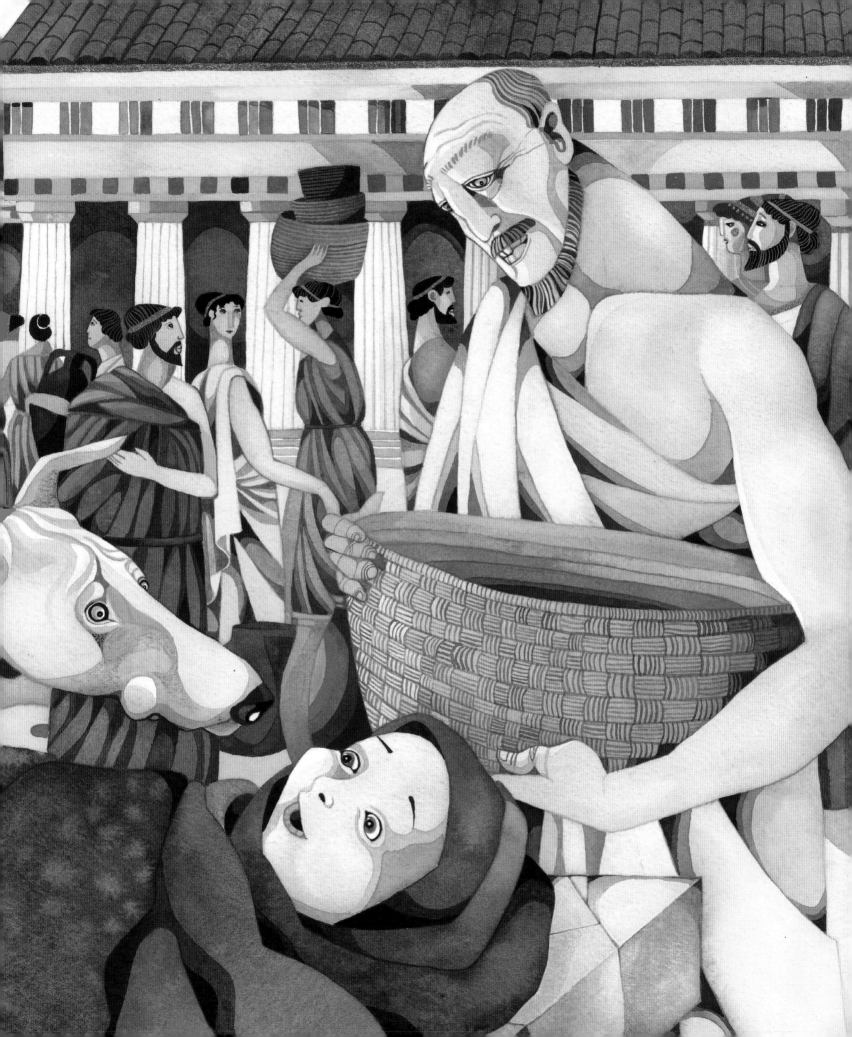

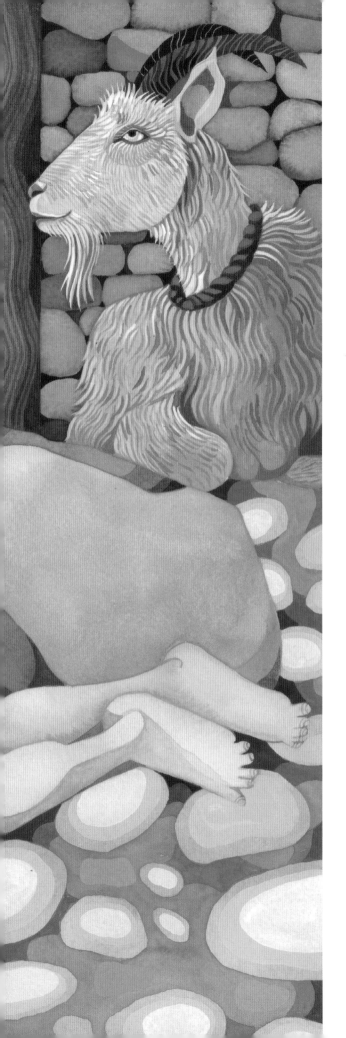

The old slave was a decent man and he raised her with the rest of the slave household. By the time she was four she had learned to fetch and carry. By the time she was nine she scrubbed and cleaned. She was fed, but not much. She was clothed, but only in a rough linen tunic and a rope belt.

She was treated fairly but not especially kindly, and when night came, she slept in the stables with the cockerel, the dogs and the tethered goats. The stables were smelly but dry and the old dog kept her warm.

The Master of the house was known throughout Attica. He was an Olympic hero called Milos of Athens and he could throw a javelin further than any man on earth. Milos had several sons (he kept none of his daughters) but only his youngest, Dion, was small enough to still live at home with the women.

Dion was nothing like his father. He was not interested in athletics. All boys in Greece trained from the age of six, but Dion preferred mathematics and writing on wax with a stylus to store his thoughts. Instead of running in the gymnasium, Dion liked sitting under a tree, listening to his teacher talk about the stars in the night sky. Best of all, Dion loved singing the old songs of Homer and learning them by heart.

A young slave like the Corinthian girl rarely had a chance to play, but sometimes Dion would ask her to join him in the courtyard for a game of ducks and drakes. Or to bat a rag and leather ball stuffed with hair across the floor with a wooden stick.

She was swift on her feet and Dion could barely keep up with her. Sometimes she would walk on her hands with her toes in the air, or dance and tumble like an acrobat.

Best of all, the children would wear blindfolds and take it in turns to carry each other on their backs and hunt for oranges hidden on the floor. The Corinthian girl was strong, and this was her favourite game of all.

One morning, Dion's father watched the children from a window as they chased cockerels in the courtyard with hoops and a stick. Delighted to see his son running in the fresh air, he marvelled at how quick the little girl he was playing with seemed to be.

Who was this strange child with such balance and speed? He recognised her but did not know her name. He also knew that his young son would never be as fast or as quick as she was. She had the strength of a Spartan and her body was long and tall.

He shouted from his window. "Dion! Bring the girl and come to me – NOW!"

The Corinthian girl gasped. She had been caught playing with the Master's son! Surely she would be punished or sent back to the market to be sold.

Dion nudged her into the main house and they stood in silence before his father.

"Girl. Raise your arms in the air and reach for the sky." She was confused but did as she was told. Dion's father walked slowly around her. "Show me your teeth," he barked. She did so. He tapped them for strength. "Now, cartwheel across the floor." She paused but leapt and cartwheeled perfectly. He studied the coin around her neck. "You are from Corinth?" She shrugged. She didn't know.

Milos turned to his slave. "Prepare her with a new tunic, new sandals and a warm robe for travel. Tomorrow she comes with me." He paused. "And you, Dion, shall travel also. With your wax tablets and stylus. We leave at dawn."

That night the Corinthian girl could not sleep. She had no idea what the next day would bring or where they might take her.

When morning came, Milos drove them in a carriage to the edge of the city walls. They entered a huge empty stadium. "Listen well, Corinthian girl! You shall run. You shall jump. You shall throw the discus and javelin." He turned to his son. "You will chart her progress each day on your tablet. Then you will play the lyre each evening to keep her spirits high and her body rested."

He turned to his slave. "Make certain she is fed and kept warm. She will train until her bones hurt and her eyes can no longer see in the dark." They all nodded in silence. "In a year from this day, she will be ready. She will take part in the Games!"

Dion was astonished. How could a girl take part? How could she wrestle on the muddy ground with the men? How could she run with them as they ran naked? This was surely forbidden? He had read how girls had been thrown from the cliffs in punishment for even daring to take part in the Games!

His father smiled. "These are the Heraean Games. For women only. She will be permitted!"

The Corinthian girl's heart soared. She trained. She practised. Dion kept watch and wrote everything down.

Milos pushed her to run faster, jump higher and reach further. With the spirit of a Spartan she became tougher. With the courage of a leopard she became quicker. Her back could bend like a willow and her arms became hard and long.

Spring arrived, the time when the Heraean Games would begin. Milos, Dion and the Corinthian girl travelled for an entire day to the sparkling stadium of Olympia, where the Games took place every four years. The vast Temple of Zeus stood at the centre, surrounded by sporting halls, tracks and magnificent gymnasiums of all sizes.

Unmarried girls and women from all over Attica and Corinth, Thrace and Sparta arrived to take part. Thousands more came to watch and fill the stands.

No one knew that the Corinthian girl was a slave and unnamed. Why would they? She was taller than they. She was prouder. And she held her head like a queen.

It was time for the first race to begin. The whip cracked and the crowd gasped as the Corinthian girl exploded from the starting point like a jackal in flight.

Power raced through her spine and her long legs pumped the ground. The crowd roared and bellowed. After three turns around the stadium, with a final push she broke through the finish line ahead of all the other runners.

The crowd erupted!

Other events followed, one after the other. The Corinthian girl ran faster. She jumped higher. She threw the javelin further than anyone. No one could beat her and all of Olympia cheered.

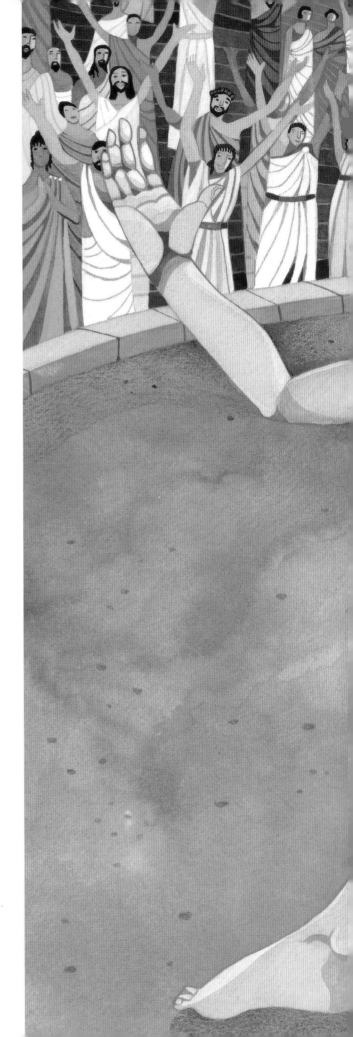

The Corinthian girl climbed onto the winner's marble plinth. Dion's father walked into the stadium with his hands in the air. The crowd knew him well and chanted his name like a God. "Milos! Milos! Milos!"

He held a torch high and called for silence. "Look upon her, Olympians! Look upon this Grandchild of the Gods and remember her name! From this day forward, we shall call her Chloris! My own adopted daughter!"

Everyone rose to their feet in a roar, singing her name. "Chloris, Chloris!"

Milos placed an olive crown upon her head and showed her where to carve her name upon the temple walls for all eternity.

AND SO IT WAS. The only girl to carve her name upon the columns of Hera's temple was Chloris, the Corinthian girl. She was no longer unnamed, no longer a slave, and the Gods were pleased.

As she was led through the crowds, a tall man at the back stared in wonder. Who could she be? Which magnificent household raised a girl with such strength and power? Then he saw the Doric coin around her neck. Could this 'Chloris' be the baby he had abandoned in the marketplace all those years ago? She was the right age. She had the same long limbs as he. But surely... it couldn't be?

He rose from his seat with head bowed and remembered with sadness what he'd done all those years ago.

But Chloris, her heart full of happiness, returned with her new family to Athens – an Olympic champion!

ABOUT THE HERAEAN GAMES AT OLYMPIA

The Heraean Games, for girls and women, were a real event, held every four years in honour of Hera, Queen of the old Greek gods. They may be even older than the ancient Olympic Games, which started in 776BCE, and were for men only.

Our knowledge of the Heraean Games comes from the Greek writer Pausanias, who lived around 110-180CE. By his time, the games were no longer held, but he found records of them during a visit to Olympia. They were held in the Olympic Stadium, organised by a group of sixteen married women, and included foot-races for young or unmarried girls, in three age groups. The runners' hair was loose, they wore short tunics with the right shoulder and breast bare, and ran barefoot.

Winners received a crown of olive twigs and part of an ox to be sacrificed to Hera. They were also allowed to dedicate statues of the goddess with their names inscribed upon them. None of these have survived. However. a few surviving sculptures also show girl athletes as described by Pausanias.

Archaic Greek statuette of a Spartan girl runner (British Museum)

Pausanias tells us that a girl from old Greek legends, Chloris, was winner of the first Heraean Games, in which there were sixteen contestants. But he adds that this is just a story.

There are no records of the earliest games. The characters in **The Corinthian Girl** are invented, but the details of time and place are authentic. From what we know of life in ancient Greece, it would have been possible for a slave girl to become a champion athlete.

Map of Ancient Greece showing the places in this story

Marble statue of a girl runner (Vatican Museum)